# The Gold Rush:
## Easy Riches or Hard Work?

capstone
classroom

BTR Zone (Bridge to Reading) is published by Capstone Classroom, 1710 Roe Crest Drive, North Mankato, Minnesota 56003 www.capstoneclassroom.com

ISBN: 978-1-62521-086-9

**Editorial Credits**

Gillia Olson, editor; Bobbie Nuytten, designer; Eric Gohl, media researcher

**Photo Credits**

Alamy: North Wind Picture Archives, 14, 24, 27; Bridgeman Art Library: Peter Newark Western Americana, 23; Capstone: 15; Corbis: Bettmann, 12, 17, 33, 34; CriaImages.com: Jay Robert Nash Collection, 11, 31, 43 (middle); Getty Images: Hulton Archive, 36; iStockphotos: Getty Images/Hulton Archive, 20, Kenneth Wiedemann, cover (bottom); Library of Congress: 4, 40, 43 (top & bottom); Newscom: Everett Collection, 38, ITAR-TASS, 6, Picture History, 28; North Wind Picture Archives: cover (back); Science Source: Photo Researchers, Inc., 19; Wikimedia: Adolphe Jean-Baptiste Bayot, 9, Geographicus Rare Antique Maps, 8

Design Elements: Shutterstock

**About the Cover**

A modern gold panner demonstrates panning in a river, while a poster asks people to come to California to seek their fortune.

Printed in the United States of America in North Mankato, Minnesota.
032013      007223CGF13

# TABLE OF ——
# CONTENTS

**CHAPTER 1**
Eureka!..................................... 5

**CHAPTER 2**
The 49ers ............................. 13

**CHAPTER 3**
Life in the Camps and Towns....... 21

**CHAPTER 4**
Booms and Busts ..................... 29

**CHAPTER 5**
Impact ................................. 37

Gold Rush Timeline.................... 42
Read More............................. 44
Internet Sites ......................... 44
Glossary of Text Features ........... 45
Glossary................................. 46
Index.................................... 48

James Marshall was photographed in 1850 in front of Sutter's Mill, where he discovered gold in 1848.

# CHAPTER 1

# Eureka!

## First Find

January 24, 1848, seemed like a normal morning at the spot where the American and Sacramento Rivers meet in California. James Marshall worked at Sutter's Mill. He spotted several shining **nuggets** in the waterway to the mill wheel. He tested one of the nuggets by smashing it between two rocks. The nugget flattened, but it didn't shatter.

Next he took it to Mrs. Wimmer, cook for the construction crew. She boiled the nugget in a pot of **lye** soap. This method was a means of testing gold. She told Marshall that it looked real.

To workers nearby, Marshall said, "Hey boys, by God, I believe I've found a gold mine!"

His excitement rose. Through the pouring rain he traveled 36 miles (58 kilometers) to Sutter's Fort in Sacramento. There he and mill owner John Sutter read about how to test the flakes and nuggets with chemicals. What did they find? Gold!

### Fact

California's state motto is "Eureka." This Greek word means "I have found it!"

**nugget** · a solid lump especially of precious metal
**lye** · a harsh chemical made from wood ashes

## The Lure of Gold

Gold is a heavy, soft metal that is shiny and deep yellow in color. Throughout history it has been used as money and as decoration in jewelry and artwork. Gold is rare, which makes it valuable. People have fought wars, written stories, and risked their lives for gold.

Gold nuggets like these were discovered at Sutter's Mill.

It is not rare to find small amounts of gold. Many rocks and soils contain **traces** of gold. But in some places large amounts of gold are found in one spot. These spots are called **veins** or **lodes**. They lie within the earth and must be mined. Over time, such veins are sometimes uncovered by weather and water. Nuggets fall to the bottom of stream beds. These are known as **placer deposits**. Both veins and placer deposits occurred in the Sierra Nevada mountain range of California.

**trace** · a small amount of something

**vein** · a long narrow opening in rock filled with minerals, such as gold

**lode** · a large amount of a metal or mineral underground

**placer deposit** · a mineral on the surface of the earth

7

## California Before the Gold Rush

Early Spanish explorers to the New World—the Americas—had sought riches. They thought they would find a **legendary** land of gold called El Dorado. They never found El Dorado, but they did establish many settlements. By 1769 they lived throughout much of the California region.

Though few Europeans lived there, at least 100 different American Indian tribes lived in the area. Before the arrival of the Europeans, they numbered about 300,000. But the Europeans brought disease and violence. By 1870 only around 30,000 California Indians remained.

A map of the western United States and Mexico from 1851

The assault of Contreras during the Mexican-American War, 1847

In 1821 Mexico gained control of California. About 6,000 Mexicans lived there. Slowly, settlers from the United States came to California. There were tensions between the Americans and Mexicans. The Americans wanted to make California part of the United States. In 1846 the tensions erupted into the Mexican-American War. When the war ended on February 2, 1848, California became a **territory** of the United States.

**legendary** · something that is part of a story handed down from earlier times

**territory** · an area under the control of a country

## First Rush

John Sutter knew what the discovery of gold at his mill meant. Crowds of people would come, seeking their fortunes. He asked Marshall and his crew to keep news of the discovery secret for six weeks. During that time, Sutter made a agreement with the Indians who owned the land. The agreement gave him the rights to mine the land for three years. He tried to get water and mineral rights from the governor of California, but he failed.

Sutter's workers soon quit their jobs and began searching for gold on their own. They did not remain quiet about the discovery. Sam Brannan, who owned a store near Sutter's Fort, wanted miners to come to California. He hoped they would buy supplies from him. Sam took a bottle of gold dust to San Francisco. Up and down the street he ran, yelling, "Gold! Gold from the American River!"

Gold seekers came soon after Marshall's discovery.

# CALIFORNIA
### AND THE
# GOLD REGION DIRECT!

The Magnificent, Fast Sailing and favorite packet Ship,

# JOSEPHINE,

## BURTHEN 400 TONS, CAPT.

Built in the most *superb* manner of Live Oak, White Oak and Locust, for a New York and Liverpool Packet; thoroughly Copper-fastened and Coppered. She is a very fast sailer, having crossed the Atlantic from Liverpool to New-York in 14 days, the shortest passage ever made by a *Sailing Ship*. Has superior accommodations for Passengers, can take Gentlemen with their Ladies and families. Will probably reach ☞ SAN FRANCISCO **THIRTY DAYS** ahead of any Ship sailing at the same time. Will sail about the

# 10th November Next.

For Freight or Passage apply to the subscriber,

# RODNEY FRENCH.

New Bedford, October 15th. No. 103 North Water Street, Rodman's Wharf.

A handbill advertising passage to
the gold fields of California in 1849

# CHAPTER 2

# The 49ers

## The Spreading News

At first people didn't believe Sam Brannan's shouts about the discovery of gold. But it did not take long before people began to believe the talk. Some San Franciscans soon set out for the Sutter's Mill area right away. Many returned to San Francisco with gold nuggets and bags of gold dust.

Suddenly, people began to leave their jobs to become miners. In the spring of 1848 there were only a few hundred California miners. By the summer, that number had increased to 4,000. As one man wrote, "All are off for the mines, some on horses, some in carts, some on crutches and one went in a [stretcher]."

In August 1848 the *New York Herald* published news about the discovery. People from far and wide hurried to California. The Gold Rush had begun!

Some people traveled by clipper ship to the California gold fields.

## The Journey: By Land and Sea

In 1848 news traveled slowly. It took from January to December 1848 for people to really catch on. President James K. Polk gave a speech that month in which he talked about the discovery of gold in California. Newspapers across the United States printed his speech. Suddenly it seemed that everyone in the country had gold fever.

Thousands of people headed to California. Travel was slow and hard. People went on foot or in wagons. Some traveled by ship. People sailing from the east coast of the United States could take two routes to California. They could sail south all the way around the tip of South America. Then they could sail north to California. That route took up to seven months.

# Routes to California

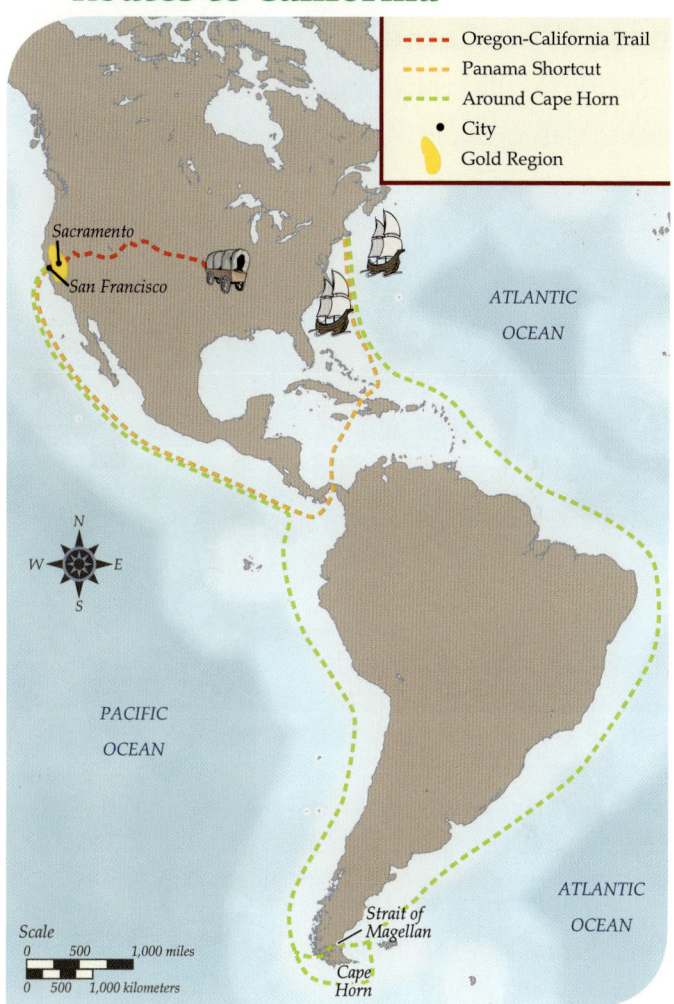

**Legend:**
- Oregon-California Trail
- Panama Shortcut
- Around Cape Horn
- • City
- Gold Region

Sacramento
San Francisco

ATLANTIC
OCEAN

PACIFIC
OCEAN

ATLANTIC
OCEAN

N
W — E
S

Strait of
Magellan

Cape
Horn

Scale
0    500    1,000 miles
0    500    1,000 kilometers

There was another route. Easterners could sail south to the strip of land called the **Isthmus** of Panama. Then they could hike to the other side. There, they could catch a ship to California. This trip was shorter but still took six weeks or longer.

**isthmus** · a narrow strip of land that lies between two bodies of water and connects two larger land masses

**15**

## Those Who Came

Nearly 90,000 travelers came to California in 1849. They were called "49ers." Many of these people came from Asia, Australia, Europe, and Hawaii. About 7,000 Mexicans came north in **caravans**. People from Chile and Peru came as well.

At first American Indians in California did not pay much attention to the gold fever. Soon, though, many of them joined in. They dug and washed gold. They also organized teams of men to work.

Workers also came from China. From 1849 to 1854, more than 20,000 Chinese **immigrants** came to California.

**caravan** · a group of people traveling together

**immigrant** · a person who leaves one country and settles in another

Chinese immigrants came to the California gold fields to pan for gold.

Some women came too. Life was generally hard for them. Luzena Wilson said, "It was a hand-to-hand fight with starvation at first." She later set up a hotel with her husband and cooked for hungry miners.

## Mining the Gold

Gold formed in California millions of years ago. Underground waters flowed into cracks in rocks. When the waters cooled, they formed veins of quartz rock containing gold. These veins were known as a Mother Lode. Over time rain and wind **eroded** the mountains. Tons of gold fragments were carried into rivers and streams. These gold pieces resulted in placer gold deposits in the waterways and hills of the Sacramento Valley.

In the early days of the Gold Rush, miners could pick up gold nuggets and flakes right off the ground. Later, miners used a simple technique called **panning** in streams. They put sand in a shallow pan and shook it lightly in the water to separate the sand from the gold. As time went on they developed larger and more complex mining methods.

**erode** · to wear away

**pan** · to shake sand in a pan of water to separate the sand from valuable minerals

## Gold Rush Fun Facts

California's largest gold nugget weighed 160 pounds (73 kg).

Levi Strauss opened a dry-goods store in San Francisco during the Gold Rush. It was there that he developed the first Levi jeans. The early jeans were made out of the same rough canvas used to make tents and wagon covers.

This 49er pans for gold in California's American River.

**19**

At first, miners lived in rough shelters.

| High Prices | |
|---|---|
| The average miner was lucky to earn $10 per day | |
| $7.50 | needle and thread |
| $11 | jar of pickles |
| $2 each | onions |
| $16 per pound | coffee |
| $4–$8 | mining pans |

**ravine** · a narrow steep valley

**gulch** · a deep channel made by flowing water; another word for ravine

**dysentery** · a serious infection of the intestines that can be deadly; dysentery is often caused by drinking dirty water.

**malaria** · a serious disease that people get from mosquito bites; malaria causes high fever, chills, and sometimes death

# CHAPTER 3

# Life in the Camps and Towns

Mining camps sprang up near riverbeds and **ravines** where miners worked. Miners set up tents or built cabins from logs or bark. Some of the mining camps had silly names—Bedbug, You Bet, Mad Mule **Gulch**, and Get-Up-And-Get.

Often three or four miners lived in one tent. They shared chores such as chopping wood, carrying water, and cooking. Men worked hard. They had little protection from heat and cold. Life was dirty. Diseases such as **dysentery**, **malaria**, diarrhea, and fevers struck them.

Sometimes mining camps grew into towns. Many towns had businesses like hotels, stables, saloons, and barbershops. Prices were high. Miners paid for what they wanted with gold dust. A pinch was worth $1. A small glass of gold dust was worth $100. Towns were crowded and dirty. Although there were some women and children, most residents were young men in their teens and 20s.

## What Did They Eat?

When in town, miners stocked up on food such as flour, sugar, **molasses**, cheese, and rice. Most of the time they ate dried and preserved foods. Pickles, dried fruits, uncooked beans, hams, and **pickled** fish were often on the menu.

Many miners hunted deer, raccoons, or other animals for meat. They gathered acorns and greens. They learned to cook these unfamiliar foods.

Sometimes Mexican women sold miners tortillas and beans. A lack of fresh fruit and vegetables did not provide the miners with enough vitamins. They often grew ill with diseases like scurvy, caused by a lack of vitamin C. Scurvy causes bleeding under the skin, bleeding gums, and weakness.

**molasses** · a thick, sweet, brown syrup
**pickle** · to preserve in a salty or vinegar solution

Many miners had to make their own food, day after day.

## One miner's recipe for raccoon

"First catch your coon and kill him, skin him, and take out the [intestines]; cut off his head, which [you] throw away; then if you have water to spare, wash the [body] clean. [Boil] an hour, then roast it before the fire on a stick. While it is roasting, walk ten miles, fasting, to get an appetite, then tear it to pieces with your fingers."

## What Did They Wear?

Most men wore bright flannel shirts—red was a favorite color. They rolled up their sleeves and trousers. They wore their hats in a drooping style. Their hair and beards grew long. Few people bathed. Many had fleas and lice. Women wore practical clothes. They shortened their skirts or wore divided skirts. **Bloomers** were popular too.

## How Did They Relax?

Miners worked hard. Sometimes they would stand knee deep in freezing streams for 12 hours a day, panning for gold. In the evenings they relaxed around campfires. They told stories about home or played card games. Sometimes they bowled, wrestled, boxed, or raced one another. They also liked dancing.

After a long day of work, miners found time to have fun.

**bloomers ·** full, loose pants gathered at the knee once worn by women

## How Did They Behave?

During the first year of the Gold Rush, crime was rare. Most people respected the property and rights of one another. The person who first removed the topsoil from a piece of river **bar** was considered the rightful owner. Miners left food, tools, and sacks of gold lying about on their **claims**. That changed as more people crowded into the region.

As more people came to California, crime increased.

### Squatters

One group that did not respect the rights of others were **squatters**. They occupied land that did not belong to them.

**bar** · a strip made of sand or gravel partly or entirely under water near a shore or in a river

**claim** · a piece of land staked out by the owner, often for mining

By 1850 **claim jumpers**, holdups, thefts, shootings, and other violence were regular problems. Some areas in California had regular or military police to keep the peace. But in most places, miners created their own system of justice. They held "miners' courts." These were meetings at which a trial was held. Punishments varied, but included whipping and hanging.

**claim jumper** · a person who takes another person's claim of land, especially for mineral rights

**squatter** · a person who settles in a place without permission

George Hearst owned parts of the largest gold mines in the West.

## Gold Found

1848 — $10 million
1849 — $20-30 million
1852 — around $80 million
1865 — less than $18 million

# CHAPTER 4

# Booms and Busts

### How Much Gold Was Found?

The California Gold Rush created a lot of excitement. Not only did many Americans travel to California, but also many came from around the world. In early 1848 fewer than 20,000 people lived in California. This number did not include American Indians. By 1852 the state **census** accounted for 223,856 people. These people found a lot of gold too. The richest year of gold mining happened in 1852. Miners found almost $80 million in gold.

Some people got rich from gold. George Hearst was one of them. Born in Missouri, he had little schooling. He did learn about mining. He went west during the Gold Rush and became a rich gold-mine owner. He owned parts of the biggest gold claims. With his fortune he bought huge areas of land in California and the West, where he managed large ranches.

**census** · an official count of all the people living in a country or district

## Boom Times

In the 1840s adventurer John C. Fremont went west. He explored and **surveyed** land, taking measurements and making notes about land features. Frontiersman Kit Carson served as his guide in the Rocky Mountains. Fremont traveled up and down the western territories and joined the Mexican-American War in 1848. During the Gold Rush, miners found gold on his land. It was said that Mexican workers regularly sent him buckskin bags filled with 100 pounds (45 kg) of gold.

In 1848 brothers John and Daniel Murphy struck gold just days after arriving in the Sierra Nevada. They made much of their fortune by using American Indian laborers in their mine. The Murphys supplied them with clothing, blankets, and food. Their camp later became the present-day town of Murphys, California.

**survey** · to measure land in order to find its borders or to make a plan for using it

Kit Carson, left, and
John C. Fremont

## Mining the Miners

Many businesspeople became rich from selling supplies to miners. They "mined" the miners. John M. Studebaker made wagons for for them. His business grew from nothing to more than $223,000 in 1867. His business continued to grow until he became an early maker of automobiles. His business lasted more than 100 years.

Henry Wells and William Fargo founded Wells Fargo in 1852. They bought gold and sold paper bank drafts. The drafts allowed people to trade the value of their gold without actually having to carry the gold. Wells Fargo is still in business today.

Remember the store owner who shouted about the discovery of gold in the streets of San Francisco? Sam Brannan never dug for gold, but he became very rich. His store made up to $5,000 a day selling goods to miners. During the 1850s and 1860s he was known as the richest man in California. He lost all his money by 1870, though.

John Sutter never did profit from the Gold Rush. He fought over the rights to his land and died in poverty in 1880.

Wells Fargo opened a bank in San Francisco in 1852.

## Tales of Success and Failure

One of John Sutter's employees, John Bidwell, did strike it rich. The area where he discovered gold became known as Bidwell's Bar. A number of other miners also became rich from the gold they found there. One of them used his profits to build a mansion. Afterward he still had enough gold to bury $100,000 for safekeeping.

John Bidwell managed to make money from his gold site.

Most miners did not strike it rich. Many had experiences like those of Hiram Pierce. He left his wife in New York with their seven children. He sailed to Panama and hiked through the hot jungle. After arriving at the Pacific side of Panama, he traveled by ship to San Francisco, a trip that lasted six weeks. He worked hard digging for gold but found very little. Prices were so high—boots went for $16—that he hardly made enough money to pay for his expenses. After a month of digging, he made less than $40. He had only hoecakes and coffee for food. He ate grass to keep from getting scurvy. Soon, he went home in defeat.

An African-American miner poses in Auburn Ravine in California, 1852.

This type of mining worked. Many mining companies used it. Soon 1.5 billion cubic yards (1.15 cubic meters) of soil and rocks were blasted from the hillsides of the Sierra Nevada. Where did it go? Much of it went into creeks and rivers, causing some of them to overflow. Some downstream farmlands and even whole towns flooded. One farmer had thousands of his cattle drowned. He also lost 58,000 fruit trees. River mud from too much soil in the water, called "slickens," buried them.

**funnel ·** a tool shaped like a cone to allow liquid to flow through it

**hydraulic ·** having to do with a system powered by fluid forced through pipes or chambers

San Francisco grew from a small town to a large city in a very short time.

## Effects on State

The entire Gold Rush lasted less than 10 years. But its effect on California and the West is still felt today. San Francisco grew from a tiny town to a large city in a short amount of time. Residents of California asked for statehood in 1849. It became a state on September 9, 1850.

As a result of the Gold Rush, wealthy farms and ranches were built in California. Many towns and cities prospered. Roads and railroads were built. The growth of the state encouraged U.S. lawmakers to vote for a railroad that would connect California with the rest of the country. This railroad is known as the **Transcontinental Railroad**. It was completed in 1869.

The Gold Rush also led to a population increase in the West. Few people had lived there before, but more and more kept coming during and after the Gold Rush. The United States became a leading producer of gold in the world. Life in the United States was never the same again.

**California Population**

1848 – 20,000
1850 – 93,000
1852 – 223,856
1860 – 380,000

**Transcontinental Railroad** · a railroad that covers an entire continent

# Gold Rush Timeline

**1847:** The town of Yerba Buena is renamed San Francisco. It has 800 people.

❶ **January 24, 1848:** James Marshall discovers gold at Sutter's Mill.

**Februrary 2, 1848:** The United States and Mexico end the Mexican-American War. California becomes part of the United States.

**March 15, 1848:** A small article in *The Californian*, a San Francisco newspaper, reports the discovery of gold.

❷ **May 12, 1848:** Storekeeper Sam Brannan sets off gold fever in San Francisco by yelling, "Gold! Gold!" in the city's streets.

**August 19, 1848:** The *New York Herald* newspaper prints an article about the gold discovery; it becomes world news.

**December 5, 1848:** President James K. Polk confirms the gold discovery in his annual speech to Congress.

**February 28, 1849:** Steamship service begins from Panama to California.

**April 1849:** The first wagon trains leave Missouri for California.

**September 9, 1850:** California becomes the 31st U.S. state.

❸ **July 1851:** San Francisco's population is estimated at 30,000.

**1852:** More than 20,000 Chinese people enter San Francisco through customs. The previous year only about 2,700 had come.

**1853:** The new method of hydraulic mining spreads through the gold camps.

**1856:** The California Gold Rush is largely over.

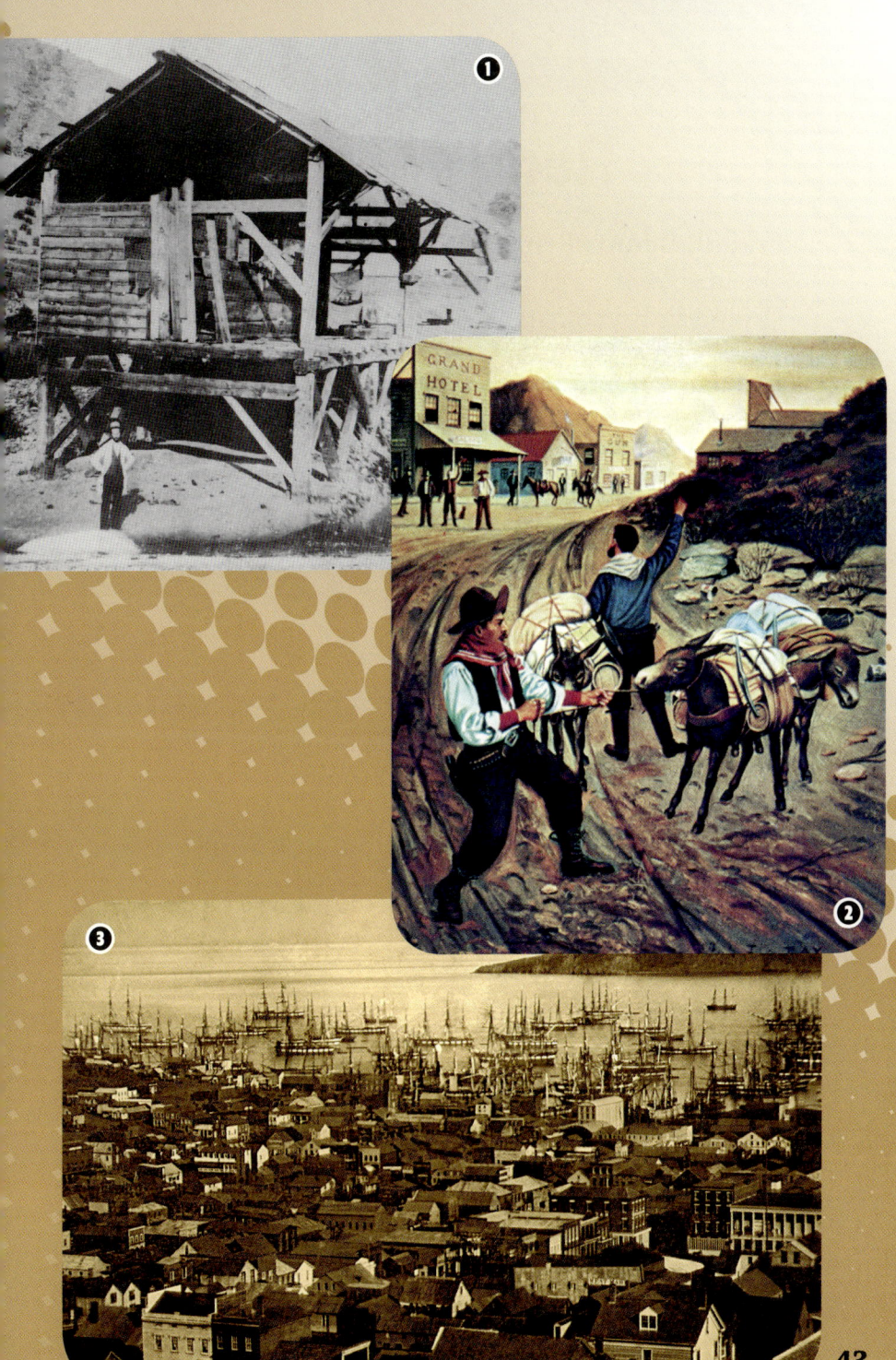

# Read More

**Fradin, Dennis Brindell.** *The California Gold Rush.* Turning Points in U.S. History. New York: Marshall Cavendish Benchmark, 2009.

**Hartley, Thomas, and Tod Olson.** *How to Get Rich in the California Gold Rush: An Adventurer's Guide to the Fabulous Riches Discovered in 1848...* Washington, D.C.: National Geographic, 2008.

**Raum, Elizabeth.** *The California Gold Rush: An Interactive History Adventure.* You Choose Books. Mankato, Minn.: Capstone Press, 2008.

**Sonneborn, Liz.** *California Indians.* First Nations of North America. Chicago: Heinemann Library, 2012.

# Internet Sites

FactHound offers a safe, fun way to find Internet sites related to this book. All of the sites on FactHound have been researched by our staff.

Here's all you do:
Visit *www.facthound.com*
Type in this code: 9781625210869

Super-cool stuff!

Check out projects, games and lots more at
**www.capstonekids.com**

# Glossary of Text Features

| Text Feature | How to Use It |
|---|---|
| **Caption:** A word or group of words shown with a picture or illustration | Read a caption to understand information that may not be in the text. |
| **Diagram:** A drawing that shows or explains something | Examine a diagram to understand steps in a process, how something is made, or the parts of something. |
| **Glossary:** List of key terms with their meanings | Look up key terms in the glossary to find their meanings and to get a better understanding of the topic of the text. |
| **Index:** Alphabetical list of key terms, names, and topics in a text with their page numbers | Use the index to find pages that contain information you are looking for. |
| **Map:** A drawing that represents a place, such as a country or city | Use a map to understand relative locations and determine where events took place. |
| **Photograph or Illustration:** Visuals that are created by cameras or drawn | Examine photographs and illustrations to better understand ideas in the text that might be unclear. |
| **Subhead:** Word or group of words that divides the text into sections and tells the main idea of a section | Use subheads to locate information in the text and understand how a text is organized. |
| **Table:** Represents data in a small space | Examine a table to understand data or to compare information in the text. |
| **Table of Contents:** List of the major parts of the book and their page numbers | Use a table of contents to locate general information in the text and see how the topics are organized. |
| **Text Box:** A box in the text that provides extra information about a topic | Read a text box to understand interesting or important information. |
| **Text Style:** Bold, color, or italic words in the text | Pay attention to bold, italic, and color words to figure out which words in the text are important. |
| **Timeline:** Shows events in the order in which they occurred | Use a timeline to understand the order in which events occurred or how one event led to another. |

# Glossary

**bar** (BAR) • a strip made of sand or gravel partly or entirely under water near a shore or in a river

**bloomers** (BLOOM-urs) • full, loose pants gathered at the knee once worn by women

**caravan** (KAR-uh-van) • a group of people traveling together

**census** (SEN-suhs) • an official count of all the people living in a country or district

**claim** (KLAYM) • a piece of land staked out by the owner, often for mining

**claim jumper** (KLAYM JUMP-er) • a person who seizes another's claim of land, especially for mineral rights

**discrimination** (dis-kri-muh-NAY-shuhn) • unfair treatment of a person or group, often because of race, religion, gender, sexual preference, or age

**dysentery** (DI-sen-tayr-ee) • a serious infection of the intestines that can be deadly, often caused by infected water

**erode** (ih-ROHD) • to wear away

**funnel** (FUHN-uhl) • a tool shaped like a cone to allow liquid to flow through it

**gulch** (GUHLCH) • a deep channel made by flowing water; another word for ravine

**harass** (huh-RASS) • to bother

**hydraulic** (hye-DRAW-lik) • having to do with a system powered by fluid forced through pipes or chambers

**immigrant** (IM-uh-gruhnt) • a person who leaves one country and settles in another

**isthmus** (ISS-muhss) • a narrow strip of land between two bodies of water that connects two larger land masses

**legendary** (LEJ-uhnd-air-ee) • something that is part of a story handed down from earlier times

**lode** (LOHD) • an large amount of a metal or mineral underground

**lye** (LYE) • a harsh chemical made from wood ashes

**malaria** (muh-LAIR-ee-ah) • a serious disease that people get from mosquito bites; malaria causes high fever, chills, and sometimes death

**molasses** (muh-LASS-iss) • a thick, sweet, brown syrup

**nugget** (NUHG-it) • a solid lump, usually of precious metal

**pan** (PAN) • to shake sand in a pan of water to separate the sand from valuable minerals

**pickle** (PICK-uhl) • to preserve in a salty or vinegar solution

**placer deposit** (PLAYSS-er dih-POHS-iht) • a mineral on the surface of the earth

**ravine** (ruh-VEEN) • a narrow steep valley

**squatter** (SKWOT-er) • a person who settles in a place without permission

**survey** (SUR-vay) • to measure land in order to find its borders or to make a plan for using it

**territory** (TER-uh-tor-ee) • an area under the control of a country

**trace** (TRAYSS) • a small amount of something

**Transcontinental Railroad** (transs-kon-tuh-NEN-tuhl RAYL-rohd) • a railroad that covers an entire continent

**vein** (VEYN) • a long narrow opening in rock filled with minerals, such as gold

# Index

49ers, 16

African-Americans, 37
American Indians, 8, 10, 16,
    29, 30, 37
American River, 5, 10, 19

Brannan, Sam, 10, 13, 32

California
    population of, 29, 41
    San Francisco, 10, 13,
        35, 40
    settlement of, 8, 9, 16, 29
    statehood, 40
Carson, Kit, 30, 31
Chinese immigrants, 16, 37
claims, 26, 37
clothing, 24

diseases, 21, 22, 35

El Dorado, 8
entertainment, 25
environmental effects,
    38–39

food, 22, 35
Fremont, John C., 30, 31

gold
    formation of, 18
    placer deposits of, 7, 18, 38
    properties of, 5, 6

Hearst, George, 28–29
hydraulic mining, 38

law enforcement, 27

Marshall, James, 4, 5, 10, 11
Mexican-American War, 9,
    30
mining camps, 21
Mother Lode, 18

panning, 18, 19, 25
Pierce, Hiram, 35
Polk, James K., 14
prices, 20, 21

routes to California, 14–15

Sacramento River, 5
squatters, 26
Strauss, Levi, 19
Studebaker, John M., 32
Sutter, John. 5, 10, 32, 34
Sutter's Mill, 4, 5, 6, 10, 13

Transcontinental Railroad,
    41

Wells Fargo, 32, 33
Wilson, Luzena, 17